Masters of Music

ILLUSTRATED BY RICHARD SHIRLEY SMITH

STRAVINSKY

Masters of Music

STRAVINSKY

Percy M. Young

Ernest Benn Limited · London
David White · New York

FIRST PUBLISHED 1969

BY ERNEST BENN LIMITED

BOUVERIE HOUSE, FLEET STREET, LONDON EC4

&

DAVID WHITE INC.

60 EAST 55TH STREET, NEW YORK, NY 10022

PRINTED IN GREAT BRITAIN

510-13733-4

LIBRARY OF CONGRESS CATALOG CARD NUMBER

70-96898

Contents

Illustrations

Preface

IGOR STRAVINSKY is the one truly "classical" composer of the twentieth century, whose major works are abiding landmarks in the uncertain territory of twentieth-century culture. Always inspired by a reverence for the art of music, which has led him to view it from many angles, Stravinsky has a pride in his profession that is best reflected in two comments in his autobiography.

Tchaikovsky once wrote:

> I have made it my object to be, in my craft, what the most illustrious masters were in theirs; that is to say, I wanted to be, like them, an artisan, just as a shoemaker is . . . [They] composed their immortal works exactly as a shoemaker makes shoes; that is to say, day in, day out, and for the most part to order.

Stravinsky added this observation:

> How true that is! Did not Bach, Handel, Haydn, Mozart, Beethoven, to cite the best-known names . . . compose their works in that way?

For sixty years and more Stravinsky has faithfully practised this principle, content, perhaps, that from the perfection of craft, the mastery of style and method, some few things of abiding value might emerge.

In pursuit of his aims Stravinsky has crossed the world from east to west, being in turn a Russian, a French, and an American citizen. This progress is mirrored in the nature of his works, and he is now everywhere accepted by music-lovers as a citizen of the world whose message, as expressed

9

in certain great works, crosses all frontiers. Stravinsky's personal career also illustrates the turmoil of modern times. On this turmoil he makes an indirect observation that reveals the foundation of his philosophy both of society and music. There is, he wrote in *Chronicle of my life*:

> the need for order without which nothing can be achieved, and upon the disappearance of which everything disintegrates. Now all order demands restraint. But one would be wrong to regard that as any impediment to liberty. On the contrary, 'the style', the restraint, contribute to its development, and only prevent liberty from degenerating into licence.

Whether people believe in that kind of philosophy any more is unimportant. Stravinsky does and in so doing leaves the world the richer.

The music examples—quoted by kind permission of Boosey and Hawkes Ltd., J. & W. Chester Ltd., and B. Schott's Söhne—are so chosen that they may be understood and played by those whose practical ability is modest. They show various aspects of Stravinsky's craft, but should be supplemented by extensive exploration of recorded works. Stravinsky's music—like that of most contemporaries—must be heard in the form in which it was composed in order to be appreciated.

P.M.Y.

1. *Boyhood in Czarist Russia*

A POET, it was once said, is one who "holds up a mirror to nature". As a starting-point for an appreciation of poetry this statement is at least convenient. By poet, however, we may understand not merely a man who writes verse but every kind of creative artist. So a composer may be seen also to hold up a mirror in which are reflected many aspects of nature; that is, of his environment. Through music the composer expresses ideas which he has inherited and acquired. The pattern of his expression is a form of criticism, both of art and of the society from which it springs.

Igor Stravinsky, who may in the course of time come to be regarded as the greatest composer of the twentieth century, has lived through a period that has seen more change than any previous period of comparable duration. In the simplest terms this can be shown by this: that when Stravinsky was a boy in the Russia of Czar Alexander III most of the people who lived in that huge empire had never seen a railway train; in the same country at the present time there are few who are not inspired by those of their compatriots who have taken a leading part in the exploration of outer space.

Born a Russian subject, Stravinsky is now an American citizen. This also is symbolic of the great social and political upheavals that have marked the last eighty years or so. Insofar as citizenship is concerned, however, Stravinsky, although owing a considerable debt to those nations to

Fedor Stravinsky

which he has given allegiance, is more properly a citizen of the world. More, perhaps, than any other man a great composer can achieve this status.

The most important of Stravinsky's works belong to the universal repertoire of music. *The Firebird*, *Petrushka*, *The Rite of Spring*, the *Symphony of Psalms*, and some half-dozen other pieces are accepted without question as part of the general cultural heritage of the twentieth century. Not only are these works regarded as landmarks in the development of musical style, but they are widely popular. There are only a few artists who exercise such a dual influence; because he is among them, Stravinsky ranks among the most important composers of the twentieth century.

Stravinsky was born on June 18, 1882, in Oranienbaum

near St Petersburg (Leningrad). His father, Fedor Stravinsky, was the leading bass singer in the Imperial Opera
House in St Petersburg, and as such acquainted with the
principal Russian composers of the day. Among these was
Peter Ilyich Tchaikovsky (1840-93), who entrusted the role
of de Dunois in his opera *The Maid of Orleans* to the elder
Stravinsky in 1881. Like many other famous composers,
then, Igor Stravinsky was born into a musical environment,
although his father had no intention that he should follow
a musical career.

As a boy, Stravinsky loved the summer days spent in the
Russian countryside, when he could hear the native music
of the peasants. Each evening as the village women went
home from working on the land, Stravinsky listened to
and learned the songs that they sang. When he reached
home he would often repeat these songs for his parents'
benefit. They were at least pleased that he could sing in
tune.

For the Stravinskys, living in reasonable middle-class
comfort on the edge of Court society, life was pleasant
enough in Czarist Russia. For Russians of the peasant class,
however, conditions were severe, if not intolerable. The
gaiety, charm, humour, and vitality shown in folk-art in
its many forms were misleading, in that these qualities
covered frequent despair and lack of hope. At the same
time they represented a strong desire to make order out of
disorder, meaning out of chaos, beauty out of ugliness.
This same desire distinguishes the music of Stravinsky.

The Russian peasants whom Stravinsky saw when he
was young were subject to repressive measures, of which
the most severe had been introduced in 1881, soon after
the accession of Alexander III, in the interests of "law and

order". Living conditions were very hard and attempts at protest were suppressed by martial law. In 1884 even the most rudimentary forms of peasant self-rule were all but suspended when government-appointed "land-captains" were installed to supervise local affairs. In the same year a government edict excluded from grammar-schools all children whose parents were below the noble and official classes. A little more than twenty years later insurrection broke out in Russia; in 1917 the greatest and most significant revolution of modern times brought the corrupt and inefficient rule of the Czars to an end.

The state of affairs that led to revolution was understood by many members of the minor nobility and of the official class. Declaring themselves against repression and in favour of the ideas of liberty as they were once expressed by Tom Paine (whose *The Rights of Man* was favourite reading among intellectuals), these people talked a tolerant liberalism and cultivated an appreciation of native art. Interest in art itself was often represented as a symbol of liberalism and there was a growing enthusiasm for the nationalistic music of Mikhail Glinka (1803-57), Alexander Borodin (1835-87), Modest Mussorgsky (1835-81), Cesar Cui (1835-1918), and Nikolai Rimsky-Korsakov (1844-1908). Stravinsky's father possessed a large collection of opera scores by these and other masters, and the first opera which Stravinsky ever heard was Glinka's *A Life for the Czar*. The abiding impression left by this experience was of an overriding brilliance, and skill in balancing sonorities, in the texture of the orchestration. It was at about this time that Stravinsky caught his one and only glimpse of Tchaikovsky, when he came to St Petersburg to conduct the first performance of the "Pathetic" Symphony just before his death. In later years, when an expatriate from Russia, Stravinsky remembered Tchaikovsky in the ballet *Le baiser de la fée* (*The Fairy's Kiss*), which, based on a tale by Hans Christian Andersen, was conceived as a tribute to a much-admired master on the thirty-fifth anniversary of his death.

Stravinsky's early musical development was unplanned. His parents, like all Russian parents of their class at that time, hoped that their sons would qualify in due course for some kind of secure (as it seemed) job in the Civil Service. Igor's general education, therefore, took precedence over his music, and at the age of eighteen he became a law student in the University of St Petersburg. However, he had been encouraged at least to think seriously about music by a music-loving uncle, and had acquired technical proficiency as a pianist. He had in fact spent more time than his teacher or his parents thought he ought to have done in improvisation at the keyboard. This, perhaps, is the best of all exercises for learning to give firm shape to the fleeting ideas that arise in the imagination of the musical individual.

In St Petersburg, one of the most beautiful cities in the world, there was a great show of splendour in the last years of the Czarist order. Concerts, and theatrical and operatic performances, abounded (though a strict censorship prevented the exhibition of anything subversive). Famous musicians came to the city from all over Europe. Under the direction of Anton Rubinstein (1829-94) the Conservatory of Music exerted a powerful, if conservative, influence on many young Russians who came to study there.

The Conservatory, however, became increasingly institutionalised and Stravinsky found more encouragement by looking elsewhere. He was especially influenced by the music of the principal Russian nationalist composers, who had been inspired by a concern for the fresh colours of melody and harmony that partly sprang from and seemed to contain the pattern and meaning of folk-art. The influence of Russian national, and nationalist, music lasted until the last phase of Stravinsky's composing career (see pp. 72f.). At the beginning of his career he particularly respected the genius of Nikolai Rimsky-Korsakov, whose son Andrei was a fellow-student at the University. On the other hand he admired the symphonic music of Alexander Glazunov (1865-1936), a composer who, like Tchaikovsky, had tried to come to terms with the traditions of German-Austrian symphonic music. The professors of the Conservatory— taking their cue from other government officials—came down on the side of law and order in music, discouraging their pupils from taking interest in many new and vital influences that were coming into music from France. Stravinsky, infected by the enthusiasm of a friend, began to study the works of Emmanuel Chabrier (1841-94), Vincent d'Indy (1851-1931), Gabriel Fauré (1845-1924), Paul Dukas (1865-1935), and Claude Debussy (1862-1918). As often as he could he attended concerts of an organisation that ran "Evenings of Contemporary Music", at which a great deal of French music was played. He also became a pupil of Rimsky-Korsakov.

2. *The Young Composer*

STRAVINSKY approached Rimsky-Korsakov with a view
to having composition lessons from him in 1902 (in which
year his father died), but Rimsky-Korsakov advised him to
concentrate rather longer on the groundwork of harmony
and counterpoint. He also advised him to steer clear of the
Conservatory, since he could see that Stravinsky's keen
intellect would rebel against the conventions of that school.
Stravinsky, when he was finally admitted to Rimsky-
Korsakov's circle of pupils in 1903, found that his teacher
had his own views on artistic discipline. He appreciated
the reasons that lay behind these views, believing then that
music is not only an art but also a science. So he pursued
his studies in the field of counterpoint, where his skills
intensified in later years, as is shown in examples on pp. 51
and 74. Music is also a craft. So it was that Stravinsky
learned the techniques of orchestral craftsmanship by
scoring pianoforte sonatas by Beethoven, string quartets
by Schubert, and passages from Rimsky-Korsakov's operas
which the master would then compare with his own
instrumentation.

All this time Stravinsky was studying law at the University, and he was still a law student when, under Rimsky-
Korsakov's direction, he began to compose his first
Symphony (Op. 1). At the same time, inspired by a general
revival of concern for the nature of Russian poetry, he was
busy on the composition of his first song-cycle—a suite
of settings of poems by Alexander Pushkin (1799-1837)

Igor Stravinsky in 1916

entitled *Le faune et la bergère* (*The faun and the shepherdess*, Op. 2).

Having graduated from university in 1905 Stravinsky was certain of his vocation. He was sure that he wanted to be a composer. At the beginning of 1906 he married his cousin Catherine, and took a house in Ustilug in the province of Volhynia in southern Russia. The ensuing story is one of an intensity of devotion to the art of music in many branches which is without parallel in the twentieth century.

While Stravinsky was on the threshold of becoming a composer the Czarist empire was beginning to show clear signs of disarray and disintegration. Alexander III, who died in 1894, was succeeded by Nicholas II, a weak man who was in the hands of often unscrupulous and incompetent Ministers. In 1904 Russia's designs on the Far East led to war with Japan. In the summer of the following year the Russians, defeated at sea by the Japanese, signed the Peace Treaty of Portsmouth (New Hampshire), which made it clear that the Russians had been humiliated. Naval and diplomatic reverses brought a revival of nationalism in Russia, but also a heightening of the demands of discontented and revolutionary workers. In October, 1905, demonstrations and strikes—that grew into insurrection—brought normal life in St Petersburg and Moscow to a halt. The government, having given way to Japanese demands in the field of foreign affairs, was obliged at home to capitulate to many of the demands of the liberals and of the workers. By a manifesto issued at the end of October, 1905, Russia became a constitutional monarchy for a brief period, and many of the repressive edicts of former years were, for the time being, revoked.

At this time technological and humanistic ideals briefly blossomed. In literature the socially committed works of Leo Tolstoy, Anton Chekov, Maxim Gorky, and Ivan Bunin, and the Symbolist poetry of Viacheslav Ivanov, Andrei Bely, and Alexander Blok gave a new direction—or

several new directions—to those who hoped for the spread
of progressive thought in Russia. In other respects men
were inspired by the exciting ideas of Sergei Diaghilev
(1872-1929), in whose magazine *Mir Iskusstva* (*The World
of Art*) a new unity between painting and music through
the art of ballet was suggested. A man of wealth and
culture, Diaghilev, whose musical interests were strong,
was the friend of many artists, writers, and musicians.
Through his encouragement some, including Stravinsky,
became world famous.

It was a disaster for Russia, as Stravinsky once pointed
out in a lecture at Harvard University, that while the
cultural forces in the country were at that time so strong,
political and economic talent was almost entirely absent.

In a little more than twenty years, after Tchaikovsky had
composed *Swan Lake*, the art of ballet had gained respect-
ability in Russia. Even when Tchaikovsky composed *The
Sleeping Beauty*, which was patronised by the Emperor,
critics spoke disparagingly of ballet music. Diaghilev, whose
ballet company (formed in 1909) was put under the direction
of Fokine, the greatest ballet-master of the twentieth
century, made Russian ballet into one of the major artistic
influences of the age, by his appreciation of the place of
ballet in modern life and his engagement of such dancers
as Pavlova, Karsavina, and Nijinsky. Not least by com-
missioning Stravinsky to compose music for him.

A composer, especially in modern times, is dependent
on good fortune almost as much as on talent or genius.
For a composer cannot be said to exist until his works are
performed with some frequency. Stravinsky was fortunate
in that at first he was sponsored by Rimsky-Korsakov,
through whose good offices the Symphony in E flat was

given a private performance by the Court Orchestra in
St Petersburg in 1907. The song cycle, also performed at
the same private concert, was put in the programme of one
of the public concerts organised by the music publisher
Mittofan Belaiev (1836-1907) shortly afterwards. During
1907-8 a number of other works were composed. These
included two songs based on poems by S. Gorodetzky, a
Pastorale—a "Song without words"—for soprano and
piano, *Four Studies* for piano (Op. 7), a *Scherzo fantastique*
(Op. 3) for orchestra, an orchestral fantasy, *Feu d'artifice*
(*Fireworks*), and the first section of an opera, *Le Rossignol*
(*The Nightingale*). The last-named work was based on Hans
Christian Andersen's story *The Emperor and the Nightingale*.
Feu d'artifice was designed as a wedding-present for Rimsky-
Korsakov's daughter, but to Stravinsky's great grief his
old master died before the work could be shown to him for
his approval. In 1909, however, both the *Scherzo fantastique*
and *Feu d'artifice* were played at a concert directed by the
then leading Russian conductor, Alexander Siloti (1863-
1945).

Diaghilev was present at this concert and was impressed
by the vivid patterns and rhythmic drive of Stravinsky's
firework music. This was music that made an appeal to the
eye through the ear, which is what ballet music should do.
Diaghilev, therefore, backed his own opinion and engaged
Stravinsky to score pieces by Chopin for ballet performance.

3. Ballet in Paris

CONTRARY TO POPULAR OPINION it is often a disadvantage to a composer to be unpunctual. On the other hand, it is an advantage to have a reputation for punctuality. Diaghilev's Russian Ballet was directed by a young, vital, imaginative ballet-master—Mikhail Fokine—who was full of ideas. Just at the time Stravinsky was commissioned to score the pieces for the Chopin ballet *Les Sylphides*, Fokine was planning a ballet based on several Russian folk-tales. The image of the "Firebird"—a bird of brilliant plumage—was familiar through many legends. The magician Kastchei was also a familiar figure (in different guises), not only in legend but also in opera. He was the chief character in Rimsky-Korsakov's *Kastchei the Immortal*. Ivan Tsarevich similarly was a frequent hero in legend and story. Fokine brought together these well-known strands into a story which had rich descriptions of landscape, a general atmosphere of mystery and magic, a plot that centred on the breaking of an evil spell, and an interwoven love theme.

Having sketched his scenario Fokine invited Anatol Liadov (1855-1914), an established composer, to compose the music. When Liadov failed to deliver the score on time Fokine turned to Stravinsky, who, now given his great chance, seized the opportunity with both hands. Stravinsky was asked to write *The Firebird* at the end of 1909. He finished the music in May, 1910. On June 25 it was given its first performance at the Paris Opera. Fokine danced the part of the hero, Ivan; Tamara Karsavina danced that of the Firebird; and Enrico Cecchetti was Kastchei. The décor was by Golovine and Bakst, and the performance was conducted by Gabriel Pierné. When the ballet was given its New York premiere, on January 17, 1916, the original cast took part, with Ernest Ansermet as conductor.

The Firebird was one of the few works of the twentieth century to become immediately popular. The music shone with brilliance—the orchestration is evocative in every detail. It was sharply rhythmic, and full of vivacity of movement. The melodies were memorable. The score was "modern", but not out of the reach of those whose musical tastes were guided by tradition. Stravinsky showed the influence of Russian folk-music; the orchestration had the sharpness of that of Rimsky-Korsakov, and something of the evocative quality that distinguished the "magic" music of Liadov's *The Enchanted Lake*. (This may also be appreciated in the colourful pages of the earlier *Four Studies* for piano.) A musical work is to be judged as a whole. *The Firebird* in its totality was sufficiently convincing to suggest that a new and powerful voice had arrived on the musical scene.

The first performance of *The Firebird* was applauded by many musicians in the audience, including Maurice Ravel (1875-1937), Manuel de Falla (1876-1946), and Claude Debussy. Debussy went on to the stage at the end of the performance to congratulate the composer, and this was the beginning of a friendship that lasted until Debussy's death.

Inspired by his success, Stravinsky thought round an idea for a ballet that had come to him as he scored the final pages of *The Firebird* in St Petersburg. It was of a sacrificial dance, in pagan Russia, in which a young girl danced

herself to death as a propitiation to the god of spring. Stravinsky talked about this idea to the painter Nicholas Roerich, also one of Diaghilev's protégés, and collaboration on the work ultimately to be known as *The Rite of Spring* began.

A creative artist is often likely to have more than one project in mind at any one time. So it was with Stravinsky. Because he knew *The Rite of Spring* to be a difficult undertaking he began the composition of a less exacting work, for piano and orchestra. In this piece the contrast between the qualities of piano and orchestra were to be personified, to the extent that the piano should represent a puppet, whose antics should so exasperate the orchestra that the latter should finally explode into a destructive anger, and in a blaze of noise, put an end to the puppet. Diaghilev visited Stravinsky in Switzerland and was enchanted with what he heard Stravinsky play on the piano from this new piece. He recognised in it the shape of a ballet which could worthily follow *The Firebird* into the repertoire.

Helped by Diaghilev and by Alexander Benois, who was asked by Diaghilev to design the dresses and scenery, Stravinsky planned the scenario of *Petrushka*: the story of a magician and three puppets, one of which is Petrushka. The plot centres on the refusal of Petrushka (who falls in love with the ballerina) to be a mere puppet, pulled this way and that by the magician's strings. The story was set in the Admiralty Square of St Petersburg, during carnival time, in the year 1830. The ballet was exotic, both to eye and ear, but it was more than a ballet. It reached back across the centuries to the Italian popular entertainment, the *Commedia dell' Arte*, in which the Pierrot, Harlequin, Columbine figures took on a symbolic, often critical,

The ballerina Tamara Karsavina as The Firebird, in 1912

quality; to the puppet plays that were common throughout Europe in the sixteenth century; and even to the "mystery" plays of the Middle Ages. *Petrushka* was interpreted by many as a moral statement on the times.

Stravinsky himself said that Petrushka was "the eternal and unhappy hero of all fairgrounds, and all countries"— the tragic clown otherwise immortalised by Charlie Chaplin. Others saw Petrushka as symbolic of the oppressed Russian peasant, a puppet under the despotic order of the Czars. As with all universal dramas, however, *Petrushka* may be interpreted in many different ways, beginning with the fact that while a puppet may not be a man a man can very easily be made into a puppet.

Like *The Firebird* Stravinsky's new work enchanted those who had come to an appreciation of Russian ballet through the brilliant and picturesque designs of the artists employed by Diaghilev and the beauty and originality of the dancing. The music fitted perfectly into the general scheme and was new and fresh, though still maintaining strong links with what was familiar. The "Russian" character helped to ensure its popularity, not least in the vivacity of the "Russian Dance". In this a repetition of melodic germs and a rhythmic energy characteristic of eastern European folk-dance are heard to pass into Stravinsky's style, where they long remained as distinguishing features.

Ex.1

Petrushka, *modern versions of the original costumes*

Petrushka was completed in Rome. On June 13, 1911, it was performed for the first time at the Théâtre du Chatelet in Paris. The conductor was Pierre Monteux, also to become one of the great directors of modern times. Two years later Monteux conducted the most astounding first performance of any musical work of the first part of the twentieth century: it was of Stravinsky's *The Rite of Spring*. Given at the Théâtre des Champs-Elysées, in Paris, on May 29, 1913, *The Rite of Spring* (subtitled "Pictures of Pagan Russia") proved the effective point of departure for what ever since has been described as "contemporary music". That is, that which shocks an audience into awareness that music itself is not confined to particular channels of expression seemingly decided by some kind of supervisory committee of theorists. Three aspects of Stravinsky's music shattered complacency: the rhythm, the harmony, and the scoring. But these three aspects, when viewed from one angle, appear as one; since the whole work is a realisation of the primal urges that sprang out of chaos into the design that we know as the universe, and of the complementary impulses that impelled primitive man to worship the forces of Spring.

The fantasy of *The Rite of Spring* held within it a kind of reality, but the Parisian ballet public of fifty years ago preferred fantasy unrelated to reality. (That art is a form of escape from reality is, of course, a belief still held by many people.) Perceiving the power and the truth of the music (which heralded the general destruction of long-held values and institutions, and a long and as yet unfinished period of struggle towards new forms) the public protested. At the historic first performance fights broke out among Stravinsky's supporters and his opponents, who were in the

A modern production of The Rite of Spring

majority. The noise and tumult were indescribable, and it was with the greatest difficulty that the performance was concluded. There was no part of *The Rite of Spring* that did not seem strange and barbaric. To choose one section more than another to illustrate the modernity of the work is, therefore, impossible. By playing the following bars, from the beginning of the "Dance of Young People," however, some idea may be gained of the distance that music had travelled at Stravinsky's instigation.

Tempo giusto

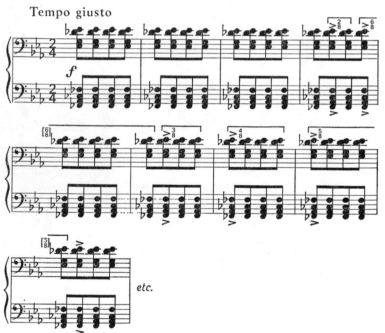

etc.

It is less easy now to understand how revolutionary this work seemed half a century ago. The rhythmic energy and the powerful dissonances shown in the previous example, that then appeared to tear the whole structure of music apart, have been included within the main stream of the western musical tradition; and *The Rite of Spring*, like *The Firebird* and *Petrushka*, has become an orchestral conductor's show-piece. It was Leopold Stokowski who gave the American première of *The Rite of Spring*, with the Philadelphia Symphony Orchestra on March 3, 1922. In recent years the popularity of the work has been enhanced by its exhilarating presentation by Leo Bernstein.

Between 1900 and 1913 Stravinsky became famous throughout Europe. The two earlier ballets established his reputation in every major city while the stir caused by *The Rite of Spring* ensured that whatever he composed afterwards would be taken notice of.

From time to time Stravinsky returned to Russia, although more and more feeling himself to be a cosmopolitan, with a special affection for France. Nevertheless, his claim to fame depended to a considerable extent on the exotic, "Russian", character of his music. It was not only a matter of association—through the references to folk-music in his ballet scores, the similarities between his music and that of Rimsky-Korsakov, Liadov, and even Tchaikovsky—but of texture and colour. Because rhythmic, harmonic, and instrumental features all seemed strange in themselves it was felt that they stemmed from some peculiarly Russian virtue. The young Stravinsky, although hailed as the leader of a new school of musical thought and also a revolutionary, was in fact the last of the Russian romantics, and the last of the nationalists, under the old dispensation of Czarist Russia.

4. *Parting of the Ways*

A GREAT COMPOSER, of whatever period, is almost always recognisable as the end of a line of development of musical thought, but, at the same time, the founder of a new order. In *The Rite of Spring* Stravinsky represented those elements that in their most vivid form had for long inspired Russian (as also Czech, Hungarian, and Polish) composers. Since the age of Beethoven musical design had centred on the urgency of dance; rhythm, therefore, had come to appear more important than ever before. But no one part of musical construction is isolated from the others. So in Stravinsky's music of his first period the directness and vitality of rhythm is emphasised by a derivative directness and vitality in instrumentation, melodic outline, and harmonic structure. The essential difference between Stravinsky's music and that of most of his predecessors lies in an absence of any appearance of sentimentality.

This brings us to Stravinsky's own attitude to the function of music. And we discover a paradox. Most music-lovers feel that music is "expressive"; that it both contains and gives voice to ideas that exist outside of music. Some are moved by the pictorial aspect of music that is suggested by many familiar titles. Others believe that music carries on from literature and that it is narrative. The works of Stravinsky so far considered lend support to a point of view that had come to be commonly accepted during the late eighteenth and nineteenth centuries. The ballets, after all, *are* expressive, giving life both to story and scene. Stravinsky, however, came to the conclusion—which he has frequently expressed—that music exists only in itself; that "it is given to us with the sole purpose of establishing an order in things". The composer's primary task, in his view, is to achieve a proper ordering of the elements of music, a balanced structure of sounds. The effect of musical forms to the ear, Stravinsky said, is as the effect of architectural forms to the eye. The result of this aesthetic philosophy is up to a point beneficial to the listener, who, if he follows Stravinsky's advice, learns to listen to each musical work as a separate and individual experience. So far as Stravinsky's own music, after *The Rite of Spring*, is concerned, it is important to remember this principle, for in a very large output there is a great diversity both of function and of style.

The diversity of the music is to be explained not only through Stravinsky's declared philosophy, but also by consideration of other factors. Of these the main one was the collapse of a civilisation, and with it the destruction of hitherto accepted values in every branch of life. The social and political history of the last fifty years has been a record of disorder. In the midst of this Stravinsky, through music, has attempted to maintain a belief in the importance of logical thought, of reason as opposed to unreason. Beethoven, who also lived at a time of upheaval, also tried as a composer to emphasise the logic of music, which led to his later quartets, for instance, being thought more "difficult" to understand than his earlier works.

Soon after the first performance of *The Rite of Spring* Stravinsky was commissioned by the "Free Theatre" in Moscow to complete the opera *The Nightingale*. One act of this had been composed before the composition of *The*

Firebird interrupted its progress. When the composer came back to the opera he was aware that his style had undergone a change and tried, therefore, to persuade the promoters to accept only the first act. This they were unwilling to do. But when Stravinsky had completed the whole work the "Free Theatre" was no longer in being. *The Nightingale*— musically a mixture of the former "picturesque" and evocative style of Rimsky-Korsakov and the impressionistic manner of Debussy, but marked with the pungency of *Petrushka* at satirical moments—was given its first performance in Paris. This was on May 26, 1914, and Monteux was the conductor. Two years later the work was rearranged as a ballet, and in 1919 as a purely orchestral work—a symphonic poem. In 1923 this was played in America for the first time, Stokowski conducting, in Philadelphia. Three years later the opera was given at the Metropolitan Opera House, New York.

The Nightingale, joining together two different styles, was a work which stood at the cross-ways of Stravinsky's career in more senses than one. Not only did he reject a style of composition, never to return to the character of the music of the first act of *The Nightingale*, but he saw that his future in dramatic music was not likely to go along conventional lines. He felt "that he could write music to words or music to action, but that cooperation with both words and action was clearly becoming more inadmissible in his mind". That subsequent works of dramatic nature were of a different order was, however, due to more than one circumstance.

Hardly had *The Nightingale* been performed in Paris than the whole of Europe erupted into war. Before its outbreak Stravinsky briefly revisited his home at Ustilug and also went to Kiev—once, long ago, the capital of Russia. Here he acquired various collections of Russian folk-lore, which were to be put to use at various times in the future. Returning to western Europe he sought refuge in Switzerland, where he arrived only a few weeks before the start of the First World War. This war brought to an end the cultural supremacy of Paris, in which city Stravinsky had made his name. The military disasters which Russia suffered, and the enormous total of Russian dead, coming after long years of incompetent government and general discontent and suffering, led to the Revolution of 1917. As a result of this a new system of government, based on the principles of Communism, painfully emerged. In the course of this great change large numbers of people left Russia, and of those who had previously left many never returned. Among them (apart from a visit as an American citizen in 1962) was Stravinsky.

Although based in Switzerland during the war years, Stravinsky went home several times before 1917. He also visited Italy and Spain. During this period he was in close contact with Diaghilev—who organised gala performances for the Red Cross in both Geneva and Paris, in the programmes of both of which music by Stravinsky formed an important part. At the Geneva concert Stravinsky made his first appearance as orchestral director, conducting an orchestral suite from *The Firebird*. Other famous figures in the world of the arts with whom Stravinsky was closely associated at this time included Leon Bakst, Jean Cocteau, Pablo Picasso, Lord Berners, an English composer, and the Swiss writer Charles Ramuz. Stravinsky found Ramuz a sympathetic collaborator and the two men formed a fruitful partnership. The first result of this partnership was the

Serge Diaghilev in 1921

French version of the four Russian poems which Stravinsky collectively entitled *Pribaourki* (*Pleasant songs*). These songs, humorous in character, inspired the composition of one of Stravinsky's major works, the cantata *Les Noces* (*The* [*Village*] *Wedding*). Based on Russian wedding ritual, this work was a long time in creation and was not completed until 1923 (see p. 41). The apparent nostalgia for his own country reflected in these works is shown also by the choral arrangement of a number of Russian folk-songs at this time.

Two other works of the period of the war were *Renard* (the story of Renard the Fox) and *The Soldier's Tale*. Both of these, to libretti prepared by Ramuz, were based on Russian legends.

All this while Stravinsky held on to a faith in the nobler

qualities of the Russian tradition (as contained in the works of great writers and composers) and hoped for a rebirth of national life. For a brief period after the collapse of the army in 1917 a provisional government held uneasy power in Russia, and with the intention of supplying a national anthem to replace that of Czarist times Diaghilev persuaded Stravinsky to make an arrangement of the "Song of the Volga Boatmen". This was performed at a Russian concert given in Rome. The seizure of power by the Bolsheviks at the end of 1917, however, frustrated this intention and also the hopes of men like Stravinsky who had little love for or faith in Communism.

Partly because of the difficulties that then stood in the way of large-scale musical ventures, and partly because he was seized with the desire to refashion musical styles, Stravinsky's war-time works stood in marked contrast to his earlier masterpieces. In *Renard* the texture is contrapuntal and divided between four male singers, seven wind instruments, strings, percussion, and cimbalom. The latter, a Hungarian folk-music instrument otherwise familiarised by Zoltán Kodály in *Hary János*, fascinated Stravinsky when he first heard it in a café in Geneva, and he employed it again in *Ragtime* (see below).

The Soldier's Tale is set for narrator, clarinet, bassoon, trumpet, trombone, violin, and double bass, with percussion. The instrumentation of this work is not dissimilar in sound to that of the jazz band of the period, and the influence of jazz is represented by the inclusion of tango and a ragtime movement in the set of pieces comprising the work. Other works having clear connections with the impulses of popular music of the period are *Ragtime* for eleven instruments, composed in 1918, and *Piano-Rag-*

Music, dedicated to Arthur Rubinstein, of the following
year. The following quotation is from this work.

Ex. 3

excessivement court et fort

This example shows Stravinsky's ability to acquire a
new set of musical values. The rhythmic structure and the
harmonic vocabulary clearly show a popular origin, even
though the layout, the extreme care concerning note-
lengths, and the change of metre, are characteristic of their
composer.

Renard, the tale of a fox whose misdemeanours won for
him the hatred of the animal kingdom and brought him to
an untimely death, is an allegory—a symbolic story. So
too is *The Soldier's Tale*, in which the "soldier", through
greed, puts himself in the power of the devil. In the first
work the story was intended to be mimed against the
performance of the music. The production of the second also
involved dancers. So it comprised three elements: a reader,

an instrumental ensemble, and dancers. At its first presentation at Lausanne on September 28, 1918, Stravinsky placed the instrumentalists on one side of a dais on which the dancers were staged and the reader on the other side. The conductor was Ansermet.

After a brilliant success with this performance it was planned to take *The Soldier's Tale* on tour. But the outbreak of a severe epidemic of influenza which swept the whole of Europe made it impossible to carry out this plan.

Nikolai Rimsky-Korsakov

5. *Exile*

AFTER THE END of the First World War disillusion and despair spread across the world as quickly it became apparent that all hopes of a "better world" were to be rudely dashed. The quick and easy antidote to disillusionment was a forced and often cynical gaiety, that led to a general exploitation of the jazz idiom in music and to a satirical attitude often vented in popular art, especially cabaret. In every respect, old and established values were questioned by the young and that this was the case was deplored by the old. Society is always divided between those who—satisfied with their own situation—wish to preserve the existing order, and those who wish to see it overturned or at least radically altered. In both cases, however, there is usually an inclination to seek for some form of discipline. Although Stravinsky would appear by statements such as that at the top of p. 33 to have withdrawn from any kind of social-political argument, the directions taken by his music, and the stylistic experiments which had already begun to distinguish it, show that what he composed did reflect certain aspects of general thought and even behaviour.

Within the confined field of musical theory reaction against size (as represented by the full-blown symphony orchestra), vagueness of expression (as in the symphonic poems of Richard Strauss for example), and stereotyped forms and harmonic procedures, had long been apparent. The key figures in formulating new approaches were

Debussy, Arnold Schoenberg, and Stravinsky. Greatly influenced by Debussy (to whose memory Stravinsky dedicated the *Symphonies of Wind Instruments*, 1920) and by the French culture which had for so long been his spiritual environment, Stravinsky held off from the more radical scheme promoted by Schoenberg, which was based on an entirely new system of atonality, and began to practise a kind of revived classicism. This meant consciously ridding himself of the obvious attributes of Russian culture.

This process was gradual, if only because there was the score of *Les Noces* to complete. A short score was ready before the end of the war, at which point the composer intended to use a large orchestral body of some 150 players. When, in 1921, Diaghilev was ready to consider a ballet performance (for the "cantata" was designed also to be expressed through dancing) Stravinsky revised the whole instrumental scheme and settled on the unusual com-bination of four pianos and percussion—hard, brilliant, sonorities, apt to the "elemental" character of the story. In a sense this work carries on from *The Rite of Spring*. It is inspired by a regard for "primitive" values—those values which could help to restore directness to music— which give rise to sharp-edged rhythms, telling dissonances, and pungent tone-colours. In this work melodic outlines are generally restricted within a narrow compass and not developed in the leisurely manner of romantic music, so that melody as such appears as of limited significance.

Les Noces, first performed in Paris in 1923, was not immediately successful. Three years later it was rudely received both by critics and the public when performed in London. Across the years, however, this work has achieved a wide popularity since it may be seen to be in sympathy with a feeling towards music which, in fact, it helped to create.

While we may appreciate the "primitive" sonorities in *Les Noces* (though they sound less surprising now than they did more than forty years ago), we may also be impressed by its classical virtues. The classical manner in art may be defined most simply as the most economical use of material. (See, for example, the music examples on p. 61.) Artistic, particularly musical, forms (such as fugue or sonata) are not ends in themselves, but means to the ends of economy and clarity. In that *Les Noces* aimed at clarity of statement it was, in one sense, classical in intention. This being the case it is not so far removed from Stravinsky's more obviously "classical"—or "neo-classical" —works as might at first sight appear. (The term "neo-classical" is used to describe art of more recent times which has been created deliberately to revive what are accepted as classical points of view.)

During the war Stravinsky had seen a ballet, of which the music was arranged from pieces by Domenico Scarlatti (1685–1757), in Italy. Soon after the war Diaghilev suggested to Stravinsky, who had enjoyed Scarlatti in new guise, that he should similarly arrange music at that time considered to be by Giovanni Pergolesi (1710–36). The result was the ballet *Pulcinella*, which was performed under Stravinsky's direction in Paris in 1920. In this work (of which the orchestral suite is familiar) eighteenth-century melodies are stated within the sharp-edged sonorities characteristic of Stravinsky's harmonic and instrumental vocabulary. Thus they are freed from the kind of deference that arrangers often pay to old music by falling back on period practice. *Pulcinella*, in a sense, sounds like an original

Les Noces: *a performance in Zürich in* 1947

work. In that it displayed such originality it provoked critics who were beginning to find that they did not know where they stood in respect of the unpredictable Stravinsky. But because it displayed a respect for tonal methods that were being assailed by other important musicians of that time it suggested that the composer of the atonal *The Rite of Spring* was retreating from his earlier declarations of modernity.

In truth a close study of Italian music helped Stravinsky —as at an earlier date it had helped his admired Tchaikovsky —to find an exit from the Russian influences that had both obsessed and enwrapped him. In one further work derived from a Russian source—the one-act comic opera *Mavra*, of which the story was taken from Pushkin—the composer took the principles of classical Italian *opera buffa* and subjected them to parody. The result once again was to perplex both audience and critics when *Mavra*, together with *Renard*, was first performed in 1922.

By 1923 Stravinsky had deliberately moved over to the field of "absolute" music—music, that is, that by being denoted by non-descriptive titles, seems to assure the listener that it is self-sufficient. In this connection it is helpful to turn back to 1914, and to the *Three Pieces for String Quartet* dedicated to Ansermet, for here one may begin to appreciate how Stravinsky began to move towards a conception of "absolute" music. These three very short pieces (brevity in itself is a form of protest against the long-windedness of certain types of previous music) are primarily concerned with musical ideas and with their presentation in the most economical manner. This is the motivation of the first piece.

The limitation of melody here shown also distinguishes the third piece which, arranged in four parts rather like a chorale, begins in this manner after two bars of introduction.

Ex.4b

In 1923 Stravinsky wrote a major work in the realm of "absolute" music, the Octet for wind instruments, which was followed in the next two years by a Concerto for Piano and Wind Orchestra, and a Sonata and a Serenade for solo piano. By aiming in each of these works at the kind of balance achieved in the classical sonata, by introducing a consistency of rhythmic pattern that reminds one of J. S. Bach, and by giving a new impulse to harmonic contrast and tonal security, Stravinsky gave a fresh look to classical virtues. In fact, by running along a strictly logical course (as it appeared to him), he was more "classical" than the masters of the classical era. Audiences of the twenties who had accustomed themselves to the pre-war music of Stravinsky found his latest essays dry in manner, and, somewhat misled by his own claim to avoid "expression", deplored an absence of feeling.

It was as if, deliberately cutting himself off from his own origins, the composer had gone into voluntary exile. At the same time his powerful gifts were making an impression in other ways.

6. *An Enigmatic Figure*

ONE OF THE MARKS of great creative talent is discontent
—divine discontent as it was once described. Geniuses of
whatever kind are frequently restless, ever critical, and
eager for change. This is typical not only of artists, but also
of those who are active in other fields. The critical insights
of such people work both outwardly and inwardly, so that
the desire to bring about change affects attitudes both to
society as a whole and to the self. The artist is usually
dissatisfied with the general condition of the field in which
he works, but equally with his own achievement. There
is always the feeling that the best has not yet been achieved,
that there are new heights to be scaled, new worlds to
conquer. So it is that writers, painters, and composers
make radical alterations of style in their work. So it is that
they sometimes go on seeking out new ways, creating new
works, long after most men have given up active effort
and sunk into retirement. Stravinsky is—as has already
been seen—a notable example of creative restlessness. He is
also a notable example of the persistent artist whose career
is lifelong.

It has already been seen how Stravinsky explored many
stylistic possibilities in the first two decades of the twentieth
century, and how he began to break the links that had
bound him to his native land. In the 1920's, at a time when
his zest for experiment gave rise to considerable perplexity,
he determined to give vent to his creativity in other directions. He established himself as a concert pianist and

orchestral director, and in these roles became an international celebrity. A growing tendency towards specialisa-
tion in the nineteenth century had left the composer at the
mercy of the virtuoso performer, whose own ideas of
"interpretation" had frequently led to distortion of the
composer's intentions. By directing and playing his own
works Stravinsky reverted to the practice of the Baroque
and classical eras, in which the composer as a performer
(this was part of his function) was the final authority on the
presentation of his own music.

Twentieth-century music presents many problems to a
conductor. When faced with the necessity to communicate
to an orchestra the rhythmic design and detail of, for
instance, *The Rite of Spring*, Stravinsky discovered how
acute some of these problems could be. A perfectionist,
he was not content until he had developed a conducting
technique that conveyed his rhythmic structures to players
with clarity and ease. He was insistent that rehearsals
should be adequate and was sometimes more demanding in
this respect than concert managers (always conscious of the
high cost of rehearsal time) approved. Because of a closer
connection with the mechanics of performance, perhaps,
Stravinsky, for a time at least, gave up the extreme rhythmic
complications that had marked his earlier works. (The
Concertino for string quartet, first played in New York
in 1920, is a convenient example to show these rhythmic
complexities in rather extreme form.) At the same time
this renunciation was also affected by his interest in working
within the climate of classical and Baroque styles.

Early in 1921 Stravinsky conducted *Petrushka* in Madrid,
and soon afterwards made a general tour of Europe. His
success was considerable and his drawing-power as com-

poser-conductor was assured. During the course of the next few years he was in great demand in this capacity. In 1924 he also came into prominence as pianist, the occasion of his entry into this sphere of virtuoso performance being the première of his Piano Concerto at a concert in the Opera House, in Paris, on May 22. This was one of the concerts directed by Serge Koussevitzky, to whose artistic integrity Stravinsky was to be greatly indebted in the years to come.

The creative artist is helped towards the accomplishment of his ideals by his friends. In time past he usually depended on a patron—a man or woman of wealth who was willing to assist the artist financially. In the twentieth century the old-style patron, like the Esterházys who employed and supported Haydn, or the Archduke Rudolf who befriended Beethoven, hardly exists. But there are a few cases of private wealth being willingly invested in the promotion of artistic careers. When Stravinsky was living in France in the years between the wars an important friend to many artists was the American-born Princesse Edmond de Polignac (who belonged to the Singer family). A benefactor of Ravel, Debussy, Erik Satie, and Francis Poulenc, she gave much help also to Stravinsky. She it was who subsidised the costs of production of such problematic works as *Renard* and *Mavra*. These works, and also *Les Noces* and *The Soldier's Tale*, were privately performed at her house in Paris. Before Stravinsky gave the first public performance of the Piano Concerto—an occasion that he approached in a state of high nervous tension—he played it through at Princesse de Polignac's home. The orchestral part was represented on a second piano, played by Jean Wiéner.

The Piano Concerto, in which the orchestral part is
limited to wind instruments, gave Stravinsky the opportunity to make a further break-through. By his own
presence as soloist he ensured an interest on the part of
listeners that began to persuade many that this stylistic
departure was a valid excursion. It began to be appreciated
how and why the composer had gone away from the ballet
style that by now (despite the alarms raised in 1913) had
become part of the heritage of popular symphonic-orches-
tral music.

In the early part of 1925 Stravinsky undertook his first
tour of the United States. On January 23 he played the
concerto with the Boston Symphony Orchestra, Koussevitzky being the conductor. On February 5 he played it
with the New York Philharmonic and the Dutch conductor
Willem Mengelberg. He also visited Chicago, Philadelphia,
Detroit, and Cincinnati. Later that year he played his new
Piano Sonata at the Venice meeting of the International
Society for Contemporary Music. A passage from the
first movement of the Piano Sonata (dedicated to Princesse
de Polignac) illustrates Stravinsky's preoccupation at that
time with simplicity of statement and a diatonic idiom.

Ex 5

It will be seen that Stravinsky was a dedicated composer, to the extent that when he discovered an aesthetic-musical problem he set out to solve it from as many angles as possible. Thus he passed in review nationalism, impressionism, primitivism, classicism, and the Baroque. And the musical material that was stimulated by these diverse principles was further disciplined by practical considerations—as of the availability of instruments—and by the relationships that belonged to theatre or concert-hall. Stravinsky was in fact a superbly professional composer.

During the period in which he was prominent as a performer he wrote a number of works which derived from his consideration of the capabilities of the piano. The Piano Sonata of 1924 was followed by a Serenade in A in 1925. In this work characteristics of Italian music, such as the vocal-style melodic line of the second movement "Romanza" and the cheerful atmosphere of the final "Rondoletto", were allowed free rein. On December 6, 1929, Stravinsky played the solo part in his new Capriccio for piano and orchestra (Ansermet conducting) in Paris. On November 21, 1935, together with his son Soulima, he gave the first performance, also in Paris, of a Concerto for two solo pianos. In this work the intensive interest of the composer in contrapuntal method is particularly concentrated in the concluding movement, a prelude and

Ex. 6a

Subject of fugue — which inverts as follows — etc.

ben marcato

Ex.6b

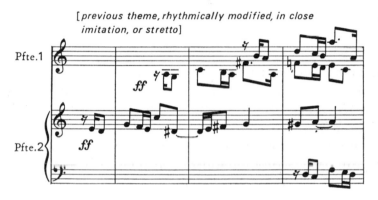

[*previous theme, rhythmically modified, in close imitation, or stretto*]

Pfte.1

Pfte.2

fugue in which devices made familiar and perfected by Bach are to be found as shown above.

More and more during this period Stravinsky was attracted by the methods of Bach—which also inspired other composers of the period, such as Paul Hindemith and Ralph Vaughan Williams. But while Baroque influences at this period were responsible for guiding the composer's thoughts regarding the structure of music in particular directions, those influences were not exclusive. The Concerto for two pianos is pianistic in a way alien to the eighteenth century (see the second movement, "Notturno"), and the dramatic exploitation of rhythms owes much to the dynamic example of Beethoven. The frequent use of repeated notes seems also to reflect the character of the cimbalom, the qualities of which had for so long fascinated the composer. Such "cimbalom" notes, indeed, are placed against the fugue subject shown in Ex. 6a.

There were other works of "neo-Baroque" (compare "neo-classical", p. 42) nature, of which the most important were the Concerto in D for violin and orchestra (1931) and the Duo Concertante (1932) for violin and piano. Both works were composed for the violinist Samuel Dushkin— with whom Stravinsky frequently performed at recitals— and both were given first performances in Berlin.

Although almost continually on tour in the late twenties and the thirties (Stravinsky's second American tour took place in 1935), Stravinsky maintained his headquarters in France, with a home in Biarritz. In 1936 he became a French citizen, by naturalisation. By this time he had, over and above the works already mentioned, composed two works which, by common consent, belong to the repertoire of modern masterpieces.

7. *World Composer*

ONE OF THE MOST GIFTED of modern French writers and playwrights is Jean Cocteau (1891–1963), who became friendly with Stravinsky during the First World War. A firm believer in the virtues of simplicity in art Cocteau exerted a strong influence on French music, encouraging Erik Satie (1866–1945) and being at least partly responsible for the coming together of the group of composers known as *Les Six* (Auric, Durey, Honegger, Milhaud, Poulenc, Tailleferre).

Some time after the composition of the burlesque opera *Mavra* and the production of *Les Noces* Stravinsky turned again towards a dramatic theme. The tragedy of *Oedipus* —as told by the classical Greek dramatist Sophocles— attracted him as one that was universal in its significance but particularly suitable to modern times.

Up to the nineteenth century composers wishing to expound philosophical ideas had usually sought texts from the Bible. A decline of interest in the Bible and the projection of ideas from other sources impelled many composers to look outside the Christian tradition. In the 1920's, influenced by Jean Cocteau and Paul Claudel (sometime French Ambassador in Washington), certain composers, among whom were Darius Milhaud, Arthur Honegger, and Stravinsky, turned to the tradition of Greek drama for dramatic and philosophical themes. Stravinsky began to envisage the musical representation of *Oedipus*, by Sophocles, in oratorio terms. The basis of

Stravinsky's work is the thought that in Oedipus there was a man who had been engaged in a losing battle with supernatural forces "always watching us from a world beyond the gates of death". Since this may be said to be the foundation of Handel's *Saul* and *Jephtha* in particular, even though Handel placed both dramas within a more or less recognisable religious framework, it can be seen that some sort of disposition of material broadly similar to the Handelian appeared as suitable to Stravinsky's purpose.

The text of *Oedipus Rex* (put into two acts) was prepared by Cocteau. Having been prepared it was translated into Latin, Stravinsky proposing that a "special language", and not one in daily use, was proper for a "sublime" subject. The use of Latin appears to give dignity to a work if for no other reason than it is the official language of Catholic Christianity. Thus *Oedipus Rex*, by association, paradoxically acquired a kind of religious meaning. The religious feeling that underlies this work is emphasised by the "Gloria" (addressed to Jocasta, the Queen) that concludes the first act. The music recalls—as was intended—the liturgical music of the Russian Orthodox Church, and anticipates Stravinsky's later liturgical music.

Ex.7

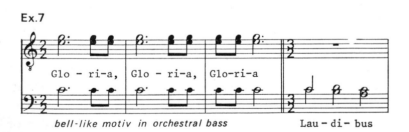

bell-like motiv in orchestral bass   Lau – di – bus

The forces employed to present the drama were a narrator (neutralised from the persons of the drama by being dressed in contemporary evening dress); soloists (in antique costume, but restrained from all but minor and formal head and hand movements) for the main characters—Oedipus, Jocasta, Creon, and Tiresias; male voice chorus—chosen because of the serious, priestly, character of its sonorities; and orchestra. The chorus members, like the soloists, were removed from the atmosphere of the present day by being masked and appearing, as it were, as living statues.

In *Oedipus Rex* Stravinsky employs principles, such as recitative and aria, that belonged to the Baroque practice of Handel's time. He also based dramatic development on key relationships and key contrasts, although the harmonies of the work are often harsh and bear little relationship to traditional chordal procedures. As always the orchestral sonorities are immensely telling.

Oedipus Rex was intended by the composer to be as unemotional as possible. But to hear it is a memorable experience, not least because by avoiding musical and theatrical rhetoric it accords with the attitude of the modern man who is no longer persuaded by the romantic garnishings of the past. It is interesting to notice that in a recent production of Sophocles' drama the Greek theatre director

The set designed by Dühlberg for Klemperer's performance of Oedipus Rex, *Berlin* 1928

Karolos Koun seems to complement Stravinsky's approach to the theme. Karolos enlarges the role of the chorus speakers and diminishes that of the principals (by depriving them of the normal gestures and interpretative tricks of actors). He also adds a mystical element, suggesting the timelessness of the theme, in musical sonorities (bells, plucked strings, vocal sonorities, etc.). In this way he too, though coming from a different direction, turns the drama towards oratorio.

The second great work by Stravinsky of this period is the *Symphony of Psalms*, composed in 1930 to commemorate the fiftieth anniversary of the Boston Symphony Orchestra.

Here, as in *Oedipus Rex*, Stravinsky used the "dead" language of Latin; but this time within its religious environment, since the words were taken from the Bible (Psalms 38, 39, 150). In choosing these words he also sought to uncover some of the simpler ideas that had been submerged beneath the accretions of centuries of romantic treatment. By setting such words Stravinsky tried not only to "let the words speak for themselves", but also, by using voices, to reinforce the meaning of the musical patterns of the work.

Within the great tradition of music from medieval times until the time of Bach musical arguments, or musical logic, had depended on the conflict and resolution of conflict implied by counterpoint. "My idea", said Stravinsky, "was that my symphony should be a work with great contrapuntal development". He added that, in accordance with the practice of the great contrapuntal masters, the voices and instruments should be regarded as on equal terms. On no account, he added, should the latter be regarded as a mere accompaniment to the former. The term symphony was applied in this case not to indicate a work modelled after the pattern of the classical period symphony, but one which remembered the broader significance of the "sacred symphony" of the early seventeenth century.

In his choral music Stravinsky reached back to earlier times, not only to the days of Bach but further back towards the Middle Ages when the meaning of liturgical music depended on form and structure more than on what was later termed "expression". He sought out the same sort of austerity and dignity in the *Symphony of Psalms* and the *Mass* of 1948. The manner in which he succeeded may be understood not by a quotation from Stravinsky, but from a Mass by a composer of the early fifteenth century, Johannes

Ciaconia. This by its general resemblance to Stravinsky
shows how far back a modern musician often goes in
order to achieve what is called progress. Ciaconia's "Agnus
Dei" may be compared with the "Laudibus" section of
Ex. 7 (pp. 54-5).

Ex.8

8. *Fresh Impulses*

DURING THE 1930'S those values which had sustained the best parts of European civilisation were submerged beneath the tyrannies of Fascism and Nazism. Persecution led to many of the finest minds in Europe—scientists, writers, artists, and musicians among them—seeking refuge and making new careers in the United States. Arnold Schoenberg, one of the most original creative musicians and one of the most potent musical influences of the age, emigrated to the U.S.A. in 1933. Six years later he was followed by Stravinsky. A year after Stravinsky established himself across the Atlantic he was followed by Béla Bartók. So by 1940 three of the greatest composers of the European tradition had become participant in a new and more free tradition—one which appealed to many artists on account of its vitality.

Stravinsky had paid a third visit to the U.S.A. in 1937 when he had conducted the first performance of his ballet *A Card Game* in New York. In 1938 and 1939 his private life was shattered by the deaths of daughter, mother, and wife. In the latter year an invitation to lecture at Harvard University was welcome for many reasons. The lectures, published as *Poetics of Music*, are an important aid to understanding Stravinsky's views on music and philosophy, and should be read in conjunction with his splendidly readable autobiographical volumes. After they had been delivered, Stravinsky—with so many European links severed and with that continent in ferment—decided to stay in the New World. He took a house in California, and in 1940

59

he married for a second time. In 1945 he became an American citizen.

Before he left France, Stravinsky composed a concerto—entitled *Dumbarton Oaks* after the name of the house of a Mr and Mrs Bliss of Washington D.C., who commissioned the work—and commenced a symphony. The composition of the latter was interrupted by the Harvard commission and so it was not finished until after he had settled in California. The first performance, in Chicago, on November 7, 1940, was conducted by Stravinsky. In this symphony, following the general pattern of classical symphonic form and affirming the importance of the tonal system by maintaining a scheme centred on C major, Stravinsky seems to reassert one of his principal articles of faith; that in which he protested his intention "to establish order and discipline in the purely sonorous scheme to which I always give precedence over elements of an emotional character".

The Symphony consists of four movements, of which the first is in the basic "sonata" form that served the classical symphonists. The second, slow, movement is song-like—also in line with classical practice—and was described by the composer as an aria. After this comes a dance movement, comprising minuet and passepied and ending fugally. Finally, a slow introduction, in which wind tone predominates, leads to an impressive and robust finale. From the historical point of view this symphony pays tribute to the main elements that went into the fashioning of European classical music, the models involved including patterns that originated or were developed in Italy, Austria, France, and Germany. In this we may see, perhaps, a symbol of American culture, which is also based on a combination of values transplanted from European culture in its many forms. The Symphony, however, brings together the different impulses into a unified whole and is a beautiful example of artistic order and control, and economy in design. Particularly in the first movement it can be seen how a master craftsman can transform and give life to the simplest of motivs.

Two motivs that are conspicuous in the first movement are a rhythmic figure familiar from Beethoven's Fifth Symphony (but previously and effectively used by Handel in a dramatic passage in *Susanna*) and a 3-note melodic germ—(Ex. 9a). The following examples show some of the

Ex.9a

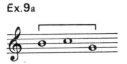

ways in which Stravinsky stated this melodic idea, and how he began to extend, or develop, it.

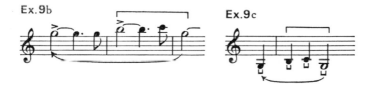

Ex.9b   Ex.9c

Ex.9d   Ex.9e

Five years after the Symphony in C came the third and last Symphony. Described as a Symphony in Three Movements, this work was dedicated to the New York Philharmonic Orchestra and first performed under the composer's direction on January 24, 1946. This symphony is of spacious design and appears as the full embodiment of the composer's classical ideals (even though it does not follow the standard "sonata" procedures), of his contrapuntal individuality, of his rhythmic originality, and his genius for a precise evaluation of instrumental sonorities. The score includes piano and harp, both of which play important roles in the framework of sonorities.

In respect of this symphony Stravinsky found himself in a position similar to that in which Edward Elgar had found himself almost forty years previously. Both composers publicly declared their belief in "absolute" music, but both were best known by works which were in one way or another to be interpreted through "programmes". The question as to the "meaning" of music which is asked by every student of music will be found to have many answers. Composers are no better qualified to give a dogmatic answer than anyone else. The reason for this is that the final significance of a musical work is determined by the listener. This was acknowledged by Stravinsky in the programme book of the concert at which the Symphony in Three Movements was played, in these terms:

This Symphony has no program, nor is it a specific expression of any given occasion; it would be futile to seek these in any work. But during the process of creation in this our arduous time of sharp and shifting events, of despair and hope, of continual torments, of tension and, at last, cessation and relief, it may be that all these repercussions have left traces in this Symphony. It is not I to judge.

However this may be, it should be remembered that external events and circumstances do have an effect on the outward appearance of musical works, just as the general climate of thought and opinion influences the attitude of the composer to his art. However hard he tries no composer can afford to live in an ivory tower, if only because he must live by what he offers to the public.

One aspect of America is reflected in the *Tango* (1942) and the *Ebony Concerto* (1945) of Stravinsky. Both these works referred back to the passing enthusiasm of the composer for jazz idiom some twenty years earlier. In the second he tried—as unsuccessfully as most other composers who have made the attempt—unify to classical and jazz procedures; the concerto was devised for Woody Herman's band, and played for the first time just two months after the première of the Symphony in Three Movements.

A few years ago Stravinsky revealed that the slow movement of this symphony had been first planned as film music, to accompany a vision during Franz Werfel's *The Song of Bernadette*. In 1942 Stravinsky wrote another score that was intended for a film—*Four Norwegian Moods*. Here he takes themes—"from a collection of Norwegian folk music my wife had found in a secondhand bookstore in Los Angeles"—and treats them with the same kind of freedom that he had allowed himself years before in constructing the music for *Pulcinella*. The *Norwegian Moods* were composed in Hollywood and in respect of his method of treatment Stravinsky again referred to classical precedent. He had, he said: "no more than followed the tradition of folk lore treatment used by Joseph Haydn in his time. . .

[the] folk lore thematic [material] only [providing] a rhythmic and melodic basis. . ."

The *Norwegian Moods* come near to a form of parody. In one instance at this period Stravinsky indulged in a rib-tickling exercise in obvious parody—at the expense of Franz Schubert. In 1942 Ringling Bros. and the Barnum and Bailey Circus commissioned a ballet piece from Stravinsky for the circus season at Madison Square Garden. This piece, danced by ballerina and baby elephants, with the dances designed by George Balanchine, was a sensation. Originally written for wind band, the music of the *Circus Polka* was re-scored for orchestra and presented in this form by the Boston Symphony Orchestra on October 8, 1943. The main theme of the polka is in accordance with the strictest principles of simplicity of statement:

Ex.10

Subjected to various amusing harmonisations, this leads finally to a rollicking send-up of Schubert's *Marche Militaire*. The whole piece owes something to the example of Saint-Saëns' *Carnival of Animals*.

In 1943 came an occasional work of completely different character. For a great part of his career Stravinsky had been supported by the faith and friendship of Serge

Koussevitzky and his wife Natalie. In 1943, Natalie Koussevitzky died and Stravinsky composed an *Ode*, an "elegiac chant in three parts" in appreciation of her "spiritual contribution to the art of the eminent conductor, her husband, Dr Serge Koussevitzky." This serious work goes straight across to Stravinsky's liturgical music manner. The first section, "Eulogy", is fugal in style. The second movement, entitled "Eclogue", suggests out-of-door music —"an idea cherished by Natalie Koussevitzky and accomplished at Tanglewood by her husband". The final "Epitaph" is described as an "air serein".

9. *Ballet and Opera*

STRAVINSKY is the professional composer *par excellence* of the twentieth century. His output is considerable and of great variety, and across the years works have come meticulously on time in response to commissions. At Hollywood in the post-war years he worked according to a carefully planned timetable, the mornings being devoted to composition, the rest of the working day being assigned to correspondence, orchestration, and proof correction. For relaxation Stravinsky enjoys his garden and is a bird-lover. So far as musical recreation is concerned he takes particular pleasure in the English virginal school, François Couperin, Bach, the Italian madrigalists, Heinrich Schütz, Haydn, and the early Flemish masters Jacob Obrecht and Jean de Ockeghem.

Between 1948 and 1951 three works in particular absorbed Stravinsky's interest, as it happens the last three works of importance to show firm connection with his own established creative tradition. They were the *Mass*—for chorus and double wind quintet, the ballet *Orpheus*, and the opera *The Rake's Progress*.

The distinctive feature of Stravinsky's composing career from *The Rite of Spring* until the works so far considered was the attempt by one means or another to reach back towards the fundamentals both of musical style and of philosophy. Insofar as the latter was concerned Stravinsky looked towards the kind of truth contained in folk-lore, in the dramatic tradition of classical Greece, in the liturgy

66

A modern production of The Rake's Progress

of the Church. In the *Symphony of Psalms* he achieved a
remarkable synthesis of ancient and modern values. So, too,
in the *Mass*, where the clear lines of polyphony, not
dissimilar to those shown in Ex. 8 on p. 58, produce tonal
effects that are austere and thought-provoking on the one
hand, but subtle and entrancing on the other. At the same
time there are episodes for solo voices (Gloria and Sanctus)
which are free in the sense that the single strands of melody
in medieval plainsong were free, with much decoration of
simple vocal phrases. That which begins the Gloria is
similar in essence to the melody shown in Ex. 4a on p. 44.
In contrast to most settings of the Mass since the eighteenth
century that by Stravinsky is marked by great restraint.

A similar restraint is apparent in the ballet *Orpheus*, which
was commissioned by the New York City Ballet Company,
and first performed in New York on April 28, 1948.
Dealing with an ancient myth—the subject also of many
operas—Stravinsky sought to give the work a timelessness
by avoiding the implications of conventional tonality and
by making use of ancient Greek modes, or scales. The
music for the most part is lightly scored, and the dynamics
are kept strictly in check. There is only one point of crisis
where the full orchestral resources are employed (a violent
chord of A minor, with a harsh, grinding, G sharp in the
bass instruments): this is where Orpheus is attacked and
torn to pieces by the Bacchantes. There are many moments
of great beauty in this score—which in some respects
looks towards the example of Debussy—and not least of all
in the end scene, the Apotheosis of Orpheus. Set out for
two horns, trumpet, two solo violins, solo viola, and solo
cello, this movement glides out of sight as Apollo takes the
lyre from Orpheus "and raises his song heavenward".

Stravinsky in New York in 1948

The last chord is one of the oldest in the book and one of the most frequently abused. It is that described as the "dominant seventh". Stravinsky here demonstrates that originality often depends on the unfamiliar use of familiar material.

In 1947 Stravinsky visited the Chicago Art Institute, where he saw a series of famous paintings, *The Rake's Progress*, by the English eighteenth-century artist William Hogarth. Full of life and movement, picturing episodes in the life of London of Hogarth's day and making moral strictures on the seamy side of that life (as the title suggests), these paintings suggested to Stravinsky the idea of an opera. Advised by the writer Aldous Huxley, who was a friend and neighbour, Stravinsky invited the English poet W. H. Auden to prepare a libretto for an opera based on *The Rake's Progress*. Composer and librettist worked together for some days until a scheme—a plot divided with recitatives, arias, ensembles, and so on—was sketched. Behind the plan was the example of Mozart's comedy in *Così fan tutte* and *Don Giovanni*.

The influence of Mozart is apparent in Stravinsky's music in the character and importance of melodic line, in the relationship between voices and the small orchestra used, and in the witty association of music and text. The story of the opera is that of its non-hero, Tom Rakewell, whose progress through life is described in the title. The moral is made clear to the audience at the final curtain:

For idle hearts and minds
The Devil finds
A work to do,
A work, dear Sir and Madam,
For you and you.

The first performance of this opera took place in Venice on September 11, 1951, but was greeted with minimal enthusiasm by critics who felt that neo-classicism had outstayed its leave and that by persisting in its exercise Stravinsky was running further into a blind alley. But the unpredictable composer, having produced one of the rare modern opera scores that may be described as charming, was preparing his own answer to his critics.

10. *Beginning at the End*

JUDGMENT ON THE QUALITY of music is sometimes less than just if only because critics are liable to be led away from precision in criticism by the compulsion of fashion. It is generally conceded that the greatest musical reformer of this century was Arnold Schoenberg, whose persistence led to the replacement of the traditional methods of musical composition by the "twelve-tone row" theory. Essentially this meant the destruction of the tonal system. Stravinsky, it will be remembered, appeared across the years not only as a defender of tonal values but also as one who could breathe new life into them. It was for long customary, therefore, to set Schoenberg at the head of one advancing column, and Stravinsky at the head of another that, by the unkind, was considered as marching round in circles.

In general the changes that mark off one artistic style from another are more gradual than history books sometimes seem to suggest. The traditional and the new exist side by side, until in the end the two coalesce. This happened, for example, when the medieval modal system was challenged by the major and minor key system; or when unequal temperament was brought into conflict with the equal temperament method of tuning keyboard instruments; or when the symphonic pattern of construction began to be preferred to the concerto grosso; or when the pianoforte was developed to the disadvantage of the harpsichord. The life-blood of art is change, and no great artist is unaware of the necessity for adaptation. For it is only by being aware of the infinite variety of art that he finds fresh aims, new worlds to conquer.

Stravinsky's awareness not only of the styles of his own times but also of former ages has already been described. In synthesising different elements he evolved a personal and unmistakable style of his own. Within this style we note the keenest perception of sonorities, so that no instrumental or vocal effect is superfluous; a powerful feeling for linear, contrapuntal, argument; an economy of means that leads to a peculiar directness in utterance; a superb control of form and, in consequence, a frequent emphasis on the purity or absoluteness of music. There is, of course much else, but these features bring Stravinsky's intentions not too far away from those of Schoenberg and Webern.

In 1947, the American conductor Robert Craft joined Stravinsky's household. Since that time he has occupied a privileged position in modern music as the confidant of the great composer—many of whose ideas he had made public through a number of invaluable publications and as interpreter. Enthusiastic for the music of Schoenberg and Anton Webern (1883–1945), a disciple of Schoenberg, Craft persuaded Stravinsky seriously to consider the musical values in their works.

In 1952, Stravinsky composed a cantata for soprano and tenor soloists, female chorus, and instrumental ensemble, *The Lyke-Wake Dirge*, the words being English and medieval. In this work then is a noticeable intensification of melodic procedure—the notes being regarded abstractly and subjected to inversion and retrograde (back to front) arrangement and then organised into strict canonic patterns. In a Septet for three wind and three stringed instruments, and piano, of about the same time a similar process of

organisation is apparent and in the fugal Gigue (the
rhythmic manner of which, however, relates to earlier
fugal movements to which reference has been made) the
significance of series of notes (with no note repeated in the
initial statement) organised rather in the manner of
Schoenberg is apparent.

Ex.11

From that point on, Stravinsky has devoted himself to
a thorough analysis of the principles of what is known as
serial (from "series", see above) technique. A genius is
the master and not the servant of technique, and Stravinsky
has succeeded in impressing his own individuality on the
many works he has composed in the last fifteen years or so.
A particularly charming instance of this is the set of *Three
Songs from William Shakespeare* (1953), for mezzo-soprano,
flute, clarinet, and viola. In Example 12, (p. 75), it will be
seen how the close-knit presentation of a melodic formula
enhances rather than detracts from the feeling of the words.
Among other works of this period that are readily to be
appreciated is the moving valediction to the Welsh poet
Dylan Thomas—*In Memoriam Dylan Thomas*, a song for
tenor voice and string quartet, preceded and succeeded by
"Dirge Canons" for four trombones alternating with the

strings. A visit to Italy stimulated the composition of a choral work in commemoration of St Mark, the patron saint of Venice. The five movements of this work were intended to symbolise the five cupolas of St Mark's Cathedral. In 1958 Stravinsky's *Threni*, the Lamentations of Jeremiah, for soloists, chorus, and orchestra, was also performed in Venice. In this work the ancient and the modern are joined together in the manner in which the

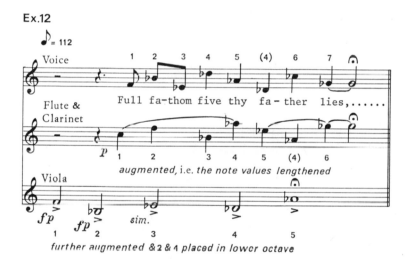

prophetic austerities of long ago are expressed through the austere and intellectual techniques characteristic of the modern serial method. For brevity, also a modern characteristic, one may turn to the *Epitaphium* (1959) in memory of Prince Fürstenberg (a patron of modern music). Written for flute, clarinet, and harp, this is but seven bars long.

Stravinsky at a rehearsal in San Marco, Venice, in 1959

Many other recent works—especially *Movements*, for piano and orchestra (first performed in New York, January 10, 1960)—are extremely concentrated. To what extent they will affect the many rather than the few remains to be seen.

And here is the problem of music in modern times. Is it an expressive medium with terms of reference that may be generally understood? Is it a specialist science to be experimented with for the benefit of specialists? Is its creative development a private matter for the composer who in pursuing his own aims affirms the right of the individual to be, in matters of belief, a free agent?

To these questions Stravinsky has given many answers. The most convincing are those of his works that are universally accepted as masterpieces.

Index

SET IN 12 POINT MONOTYPE GARAMOND AND
PRINTED IN GREAT BRITAIN
BY THE PRESS AT COOMBELANDS LIMITED
ADDLESTONE, SURREY